Contents

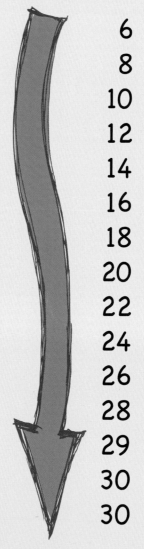

At the playground

Playground rides are fun to use.

Which playground equipment do you like?

Zhane and Finlaye like the swings.

Finlaye also has fun on the climbing frame.

6

Match these names to the rides in the pictures.

Seesaw
Roundabout
Rocker

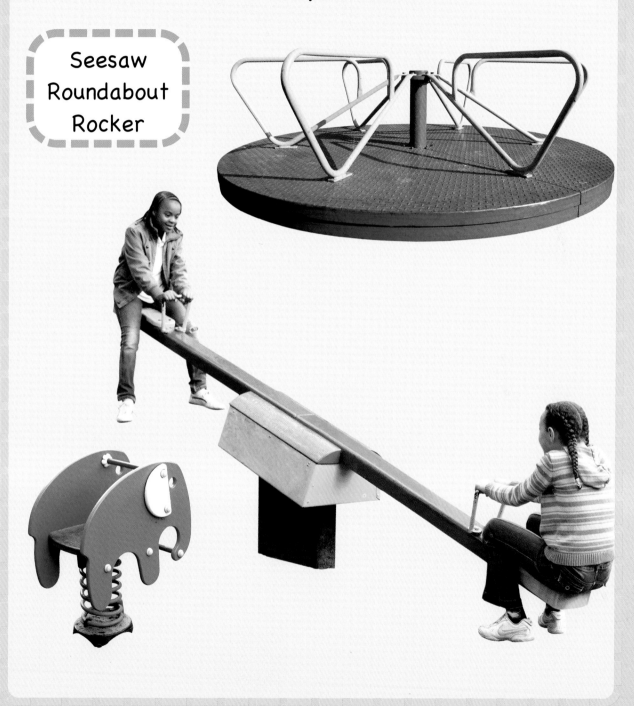

Playground shapes

What different shapes can you see in the playground?

The wheels on this toy train are circle shapes.

This climbing frame is made up of triangles.

8

A framework holds things up. Shapes with a wide base make stable frameworks.

The frame for these swings have triangle ends. Triangles are wide at the base.

What other shapes can you see in this climbing frame?

Make a slide

Toolbox
- Scissors • Card
- Tape • Plastic bricks

Finton is making a slide. He makes the ladder from plastic bricks.

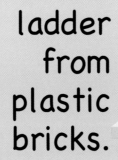

He makes sure the steps of the ladder are evenly spaced.

He measures and cuts a piece of card for the slide.

Finton bends the card
to make the slide.
He joins this to the
ladder with tape.
What else could
he use?

What shape
does the slide
framework
make with
the ground?

How has Finton made the
slide model even safer?

Safety note:
Take care with
scissors.

Pushes and pulls

Forces make playground rides move. Forces are pushes and pulls.

Finlaye pushes the swing to start it moving.

Zhane pulls on the bars to stop the roundabout turning.

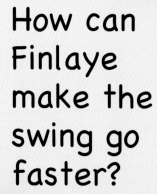

How can Finlaye make the swing go faster?

Forces make different kinds of movement. Swings move back and forth. Seesaws move up and down.

What words describe the way these playground rides move?

Make a  seesaw

Curtis makes a seesaw.

He cuts out two long rectangles of card the same size. He glues them together. This makes a strong, stiff seesaw plank.

Curtis cuts out two eggboxes to make seats. He paints the boxes yellow.

Next, Curtis glues the eggboxes to each end of the plank.

He tapes the plank across a cylinder-shaped tin.

When Curtis puts a heavier toy at one end, the weight pushes that end down. This force makes the other end go up!

Toolbox
- Card • Ruler
- Scissors • Glue
- Paint • Large cylinder

What will happen if Curtis puts on two toys of the same weight?

Playground **materials**

Playground rides are made of different materials.

This swing seat is plastic. It is strong and waterproof.

This slide is made from smooth metal.

This chart shows the different materials in a playground. Why were these chosen? Which is used most?

MATERIALS		
Metal	Wood	Plastic
Chain	Seat	Seat
Frame	Frame	Slide
Screws	Train	Rocker
Slide		

Playground materials are joined together in different ways.

The metal parts of this rung have been melted together.

The metal chain on this swing is joined together in links.

Make a **roundabout**

Charlie makes a roundabout. First, he pokes a pencil through the middle of a paper plate.

Next, Charlie paints his roundabout yellow to make it look like plastic.

How could he make it look like metal?

Charlie sticks the pencil through the plate into Plasticine.

Then he slides a straw over the pencil.

Charlie bends pipe cleaners to make bars. He tapes them to the straw and the plate edge.

Toolbox
- Paper plate • Pencil
- Straw • Paints • Plasticine
- Tape • Scissors
- Pipe cleaners

What should happen when Charlie pushes the bars?

Playground design

Some playgrounds are designed for older children. Others are designed for very young children.

Who do you think this playground is for? Why?

What is the theme of this playground?

What playground would you design and draw?

20

Playground equipment is designed to be safe.

The sides on this slide stop children falling off.

Why do you think this playground floor is soft and springy?

What safety rules would you make for the playground?

Planning a **swing**

Simran plans a swing for a baby. Which of these swings is best for babies?

String   Egg box

Simran labels the parts of her design with the materials she will use.

Straws

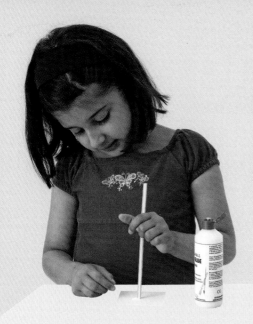

Simran tries different methods of joining the materials.

She glues the ends of the straws to card.

She flattens the end of one straw to stick it to another.

She joins two straws with a pipe cleaner. Which method do you think she will use to make the swing? Turn the page to find out.

Making the **swing**

Simran joins three straws with pipe-cleaners to make a frame. She makes another frame and joins the two together with tape.

She uses a hole punch to make holes in the egg box seat.

She threads string through these holes and ties it to the top bar. Then she tries her swing out with her toy rabbit.

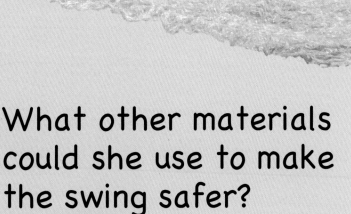

Simran puts Plasticine under the swing to make it more secure. She puts bubble wrap underneath it to make the floor safer.

What other materials could she use to make the swing safer?

What do you  know?

What different
materials
are these
playground rides
made from?

Make a chart to organise
the information.
(Look at page 16 for ideas.)

What is your favourite ride?

This bar graph shows the choices made by a class. What was the favourite ride? How many people chose the jungle gym?

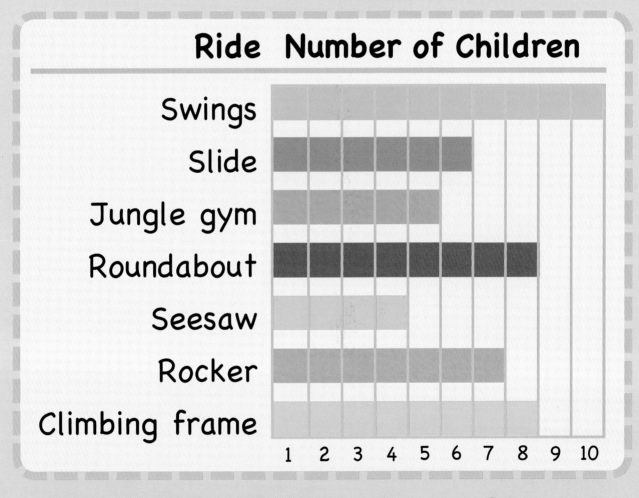

Ride   Number of Children

Ride	
Swings	
Slide	
Jungle gym	
Roundabout	
Seesaw	
Rocker	
Climbing frame	

1 2 3 4 5 6 7 8 9 10

Do a survey of your class to find out everyone's favourite ride. Make a chart with the results.

Useful words

Bar graph – a kind of graph that uses bars of different lengths to compare different numbers of things.

Design - to plan and draw something and decide what materials should be used to make it.

Equipment - an object we use to do something, for example, a tool like a hammer or a seesaw in a playground.

Force - a force is a push or a pull. We use forces to do many things, from opening a book to riding a bike.

Framework - the part that forms the shape of an object and holds it up.

Materials - things we need to make something. Plastic, fabric, metal and wood are all materials.

Method - way of doing something.

Model - a model is a small version of a larger object. A model is not flat like a picture. A model has width, depth and height.

Rule - a rule is a statement telling us how to behave. Rules are often there to keep us safe, for example on the road.

Stable - when something is stable it stands up strong and does not tip or topple over.

Survey - a survey is a way of gathering information. Surveys often ask lots of different people the same question, such as 'What is your favourite fruit?.'

Theme - an idea or subject. The theme of this book is playgrounds.

Waterproof – when something is waterproof it does not let water pass through it.

Some answers

Here are some answers to the questions we have asked in this book. Don't worry if you had some different answers to ours; you may be right, too. Talk through your answer with other people and see if you can explain why it is right.

p.9   A rectangle and a triangle.

p.11   He could use Plasticine.
It makes a triangle shape.
He has used pipe-cleaners to make safety bars.

p.12   Finlaye could push the swing harder.

p.13   Roundabouts go round and round and a rocker moves backwards and forwards.

p.15   The seesaw would balance.

p.16   The materials have been chosen for a variety of reasons, including their strength and whether or not they are waterproof.
Metal is used the most.

p.18   He could paint it blue or grey or cover it in foil.

p.19   The roundabout should move round.

p.20   This playground is for young children. The rides are all close to the ground and there is a soft, sandy floor.
The theme is the sea.

p.21   The floor is soft and springy to make it safer to land on.

p.25   Woodchips.

p.26   The swing is made from metal and plastic, the roundabout is made from metal and wood, the seesaw is made from wood and metal, the slide is made from plastic and the rocker is made from plastic, metal and wood.

p.27   The favourite ride is the swings.
Five people chose the jungle gym.

Index

About this book

Ways into Technology is designed to encourage children to think about the way the things in their world are designed and made. Playgrounds are a popular topic for this age group and an easy and familiar one for children to think and talk about.

• Even if you cannot visit a playground, in an introductory discussion the children will still have views about why we have playgrounds, who they are for and what playground rides are fun to use.

• Working through the book will introduce ideas about designing for particular groups, thinking about the materials used in equipment, why those materials are used and how those materials are joined. In discussing materials on pages 16–17 you could introduce the word properties and extend their ideas about the way materials are chosen because of their different properties. They could also discuss why playground rides are waterproof and why they have to be strong.

• Thinking about the way different things in a playground move is an opportunity to discuss forces and movement. This can start with simpler concepts, such as pushing a swing, but you could move on to more tricky ones, such as gravity that pulls us down a slide.

• When the children finish models and test them, either by putting a toy figure inside them (as on pp24–25) or simply by pulling on them a bit, they can try out different methods of reinforcing models, such as adding Plasticine to the bases, adding additional strips of card, or triangular pieces of card to corners.